RPA FOR
EVERYONE

Robotic Process Automation, this famous unknown

by **Vincenzo Marchica**

Founder and CEO of the Vincix Group, Vincenzo was one of the first to adopt RPA. He is one of the few people in the industry who can genuinely claim to have more than a decade of real experience in the RPA world. He is an experienced professional with a clear focus on solving business problems through new technologies.

Founder, Ambassador and Vice President of RPA Italy
Chief Evangelist of Vincix Group

1

Preface

Robotic Process Automation, this famous unknown...

We talk a lot about Digital Transformation, Digital workforce, Intelligence Automation, Robotic Process Automation, Hyperautomation... in short, there is a lot of talk about innovation.

By "RPA for everyone" I don't mean that RPA can be carried out by anyone, quite the opposite! Process automation is a serious matter and should be entrusted to experienced professionals. The fact that RPA seems simple leads often to an approximate and simple approach.

In this book, I expose the story of my career in the world of RPA, I present my point of view, beginning with when I started in 2008 until today (2020), and I will give hints, additional information, and practical advice on how to proceed in this journey.

I hope it will be useful to all the protagonists of the RPA world, from the merely curious ones to the programmers or RPA architects, finishing with those in charge of procedures in the corporate world. To sum up, to all those who want to learn more about the world of process automation.

Summary

Acknowledgements

Firstly, I would like to thank my wife Maria Cristina, who has supported me, incited and "endured" me all these years. She was the only one who believed and supported me when, in 2016, I left a good job and an excellent position to pursue my passion... a company that would take care of RPA. To most people, it seemed like a lost bet at the beginning... but not to her. For everything she has done in the past and for what she will endure in the future... thank you very much!

The second thank you goes to my business partners, Marco and Giovanni, who have believed in me, helped me so much, and with whom I face this fantastic journey that is the Vincix Group.

My third thank goes to Roberto, who introduced me to the fantastic world of RPA in 2008.

Other thanks are scattered throughout the book... because, in these long years, I have had the good fortune to gather many teachings and ideas from my experiences that have brought me here...

Last but not least is for my son, who designed the logo of the company.

RPA for everyone – by Vincenzo Marchica

Part one

THE STRANGE PATH

Chapter 1 - The origins

If, as a child, I had been told that when I was forty years old, I would have worked in my own company, and in the development of RPA systems, I would have gladly put a thousand signatures on it while ignoring what RPA could mean. In the Nineties, my "computerized" experience was the Amiga 500, which was slowly replacing the legendary Commodore 64; I still remember the minutes of waiting in loading a game, an endless time I spent chatting with friends until finally, the home screen would say that we could start.

All these things now seem prehistoric, but we are only talking about twenty years ago. Technology has made great strides forward, and now it's unthinkable even to wait a few seconds for an app to open on your smartphone: if this happens, the app is soon deleted from the device. The speed of change has led to a new way of living and working.

My path towards RPA begins, unwittingly, with the choice of the university course. At the end of the scientific high school, I asked my father for advice on which course could have been more appropriate considering my school career up to that point. My father, in a very democratic way, told me that I could choose any course in the Engineering department that I wanted... I voluntarily accepted this "fake" freedom, also because I had guessed that the

5

only faculty able to give me a future and an almost certain career was that one.

My memories as a child first and then as a boy, are linked to a series of facts which, a few years later, made me understand how I already had an inclination for entrepreneurial activity since I was a child and, in general, for selling something of mine and making some money out of it to take some personal satisfaction away from me. A few examples may clarify what I have just said.

One day, when I was seven or eight years old, I went out to buy a trumpet for my bike. I bought one for five thousand lire. On my way back home, a friend of mine noticed the trumpet and said, "How beautiful this trumpet is!". I don't know what came to my mind when I heard that comment. The fact is that I proposed to sell it at a "very reasonable" price: eight thousand lire. He accepted and gave me the money. So, once I had cashed in the money from my first sale, I went back to the shop, I bought another trumpet for five thousand lire and kept the rest of the money in my pocket, which at that time was a modest gain for a child of my age.

Another fun fact I remember is when I receive a hamster as a gift. When I had to choose a second one, I studied the situation and realized that a hamster generates more hamsters at the rate of five to six every three months. I knew that the shopkeeper was selling the hamster cubs at ten thousand lire each. I stepped forward and told the shopkeeper if he was willing to pay me if I brought him more baby hamsters. We agreed on a sum of four thousand lire per puppy, and this hypothetical sum was such a massive stimulus that in a few months, I had about thirty puppies. Every month I was selling about ten puppies.

RPA for everyone – by Vincenzo Marchica

Putting together my passion for Engineering and this propensity for sales and entrepreneurship, I was able to follow a well-defined training path in which I certainly put a lot of effort. An intense and pleasant study, all linked to the desire to work as an entrepreneur. Step by step, I cultivated my passion for everything related to technology, following, at first, only the idea of being able to have fun with it and realizing later that everything could become the cornerstone of my professional career.

I don't tell these things so that the reader will be impressed by my sagacity and goodwill, but to make them understand that my idea of work was based - and it is still based - on the idea of doing something to satisfy the needs and requirements of others.

In September 1998, I enrolled in the Faculty of Engineering, and a few weeks later, I joined the "engineering club". The club used to organize several meetings, such as the one where a representative of a school, based in Rome, came to present the training activities. That was the ELIS school, a multi-school reality that helps to train students in various fields, including the technological one.

I noticed that the ELIS Consortium was about to start a professional course called "Multimedia Languages and Technologies" that would have last two years. The course had a very intensive program and involved teaching a whole range of programming and video editing languages and 3D techniques. I was really attracted to this course. Also, because at that time in Palermo, there were no similar courses able to provide me with those skills that I considered fundamental to start moving my career. I sent the application, and I was invited for an interview at the headquarters. They only took twenty-eight students, and that

RPA for everyone – by Vincenzo Marchica

year there were sent about four hundred applications. I was selected as one of the participants. I started the course in Rome, keeping my university enrollment active. In June 2000, I passed my last exams at the University of Palermo. I asked for a transfer to the Computer Engineering courses at the "La Sapienza" the University of Rome, and in September 2000, I started my period in the Capital, a period that would incredibly extend until the present.

Chapter 2 - From Palermo to Rome

In my professional experience, at least in the beginning, ELIS was fundamental because it allowed me to take flight into the world of work.

I had my first job opportunity at Rai.Net. At the end of that period, I had no intention of remaining with Rai. I wasn't the guy with the fixation on the "permanent position" at Checco Zalone's movies.

Immediately afterwards, I started working for a Roman company as a web developer. My boss was Stefano Epifani, who is now an important university lecturer and journalist, and since 2016 has been president of the "Digital Transformation Institute". We worked as consultants for large companies. I owe him my entry into the world of entrepreneurial work. I learned a lot during those years, how to deal with clients, suppliers, and collaborators... how to manage difficult situations and commercial negotiations. Obviously, I made dozens of mistakes during those years, and he was always there to correct me and explain to me how to improve.

RPA for everyone – by Vincenzo Marchica

I can say that in my first experience, I immediately learned that innovation, change, and continuous training are essential components for the success of a company but also of a professional.

I would have a thousand exciting stories to tell about the time I worked with Stefano, but one, in particular, has stuck with me. It was during a business meeting where we were presenting our platform, the client asked a series of questions and if we included a very incredibly complex function. Stefano didn't get upset. He answered yes and also explained this function in detail, why we introduced it to the platform and which were the advantages! I was listening to him, smiling and nodding. After the meeting, I approached Stefano and whispered to him: "Ste, but I've never done that function" he turned to me and said, "I know, but we have all weekend to prepare it... and remember that nothing is impossible, you just have to want it". The function was online and available the following Monday!

A few months later, I went for an interview at the Pontifical University of the Holy Cross, and everything went well, despite an episode that didn't put me in a good mood. At a certain point, they asked me if I knew what a video matrix was. I answered that, if I put the two terms together, I could have imagined it, but I didn't realise that the video matrix was an analogue video tool. When they asked me if I had already worked with video matrices, I replied that I had never done so but that I would have studied it in a manual if they had given one to me. Perhaps it was this answer, decisive and sincere, that decreed the fate of that interview. I was hired on a part-time contract.

It was a beautiful experience for me because I was learning that job day after day. I always saw the world of work as something where I had to have fun and feel good, working to achieve a goal with the hope of not getting bored. I don't think it's effortless to do something like this, mainly because often, what someone wants and what someone does, rarely happens. From this point of view, I have been lucky and very determined not to be burdened by the routine of a job that is always the same and an end in itself. That job at PUSC gave me the chance to train, to go to work cheerfully and to experiment with new things to improve and increase my professional prestige.

During that same period, I also continued to work with Stefano Epifani. One line of activity I followed with him was online distance learning. At that time, and it was nearly 2002, there were no platforms dedicated to this service. Stefano had fully identified a beautiful emerging need. In the following years, I did several jobs and opened an IT consulting company, the "IT Consulting" but because it's not too relevant to this book I'll skip to 2008.

Chapter 3 - The origins of RPA

In 2008, RPA was still not called like this. We owe the term to Pat Geary of Blue Prism who invented the term Robotic Process Automation in 2012 before that time it was usually called Business Process Automation.

I had the pleasure of meeting Pat in London during the Blue Prism World event in 2017, but it wasn't until 2020 that I had the enormous thrill of having a beer with him and Jason Kingdon (CEO of BP).

Figure 1 - With Pat Geary and Jason Kingdon - London 2020

It's common to imagine that the leading RPA vendors were born recently, but in fact, they are all relatively far back in time. The

RPA for everyone – by Vincenzo Marchica

first to be born was Blue Prism, in 2001, followed by Automation Anywhere in 2003 and Automate (2004) and UiPath (2005).

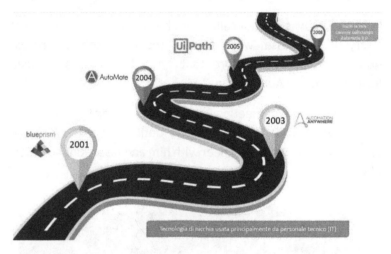

At that time, the technology was used and designed for technical staff, and in the companies, it was used and welcomed by the IT department. This method was one of the main factors that kept this technology unknown to most of the people for many years.

In 2012, Pat Geary conceived the term RPA, and the market wakes up!

The pivotal point is that, after that moment, RPA is brought to the tables of Business owners and no longer IT, and they start to understand, to do this practice on their own and discover that it can promptly implement a lot of things. The fuse now is lit!

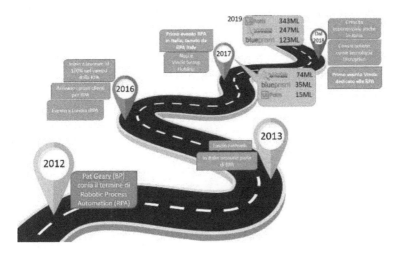

Figure 2 - Roadmap post-2012

In the Roadmap post-2012, I report the following milestones:

- 2012: Pat Geary coined the term RPA
- 2013: Very few people talk about RPA in Italy, even though I left Fastweb that year after almost five years of automated developments and processes.
- 2016: I start working full-time in the RPA field, and the first big clients begin to arrive. I attend the IRPA AI event in London.
- 2017: First RPA event in Italy organized by my association RPA Italy.
- 2018: RPA begins to overgrow in Italy too and is consecrated globally as a disruptive technology.

RPA for everyone – by Vincenzo Marchica

- 2019: RPA's leading vendors record exponential sales growth.

Concerning the turnover of the leading RPA vendors, I report below a chart to highlight the impressive growth they recorded from 2017 to 2019.

Here is the development of the three leading players: Blue Prism, Automation Anywhere and UiPath.

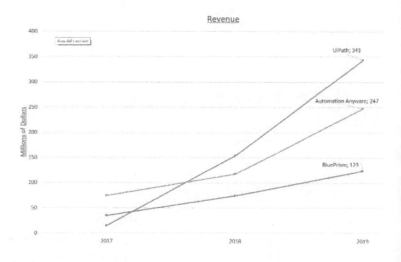

To better understand how these events have influenced my path and how they intertwine with the recent history of RPA in my life and Italy, it is necessary to take a few steps back in time.

In 2008 I was called for an interview at Fastweb.

I went to the interview, and my future boss told me that Fastweb was planning to set up a new office and that, based on my résumé, I could have a useful initial background to do the job in the right way. The new office that they were setting up would have focused on process automation. When they asked me if I knew what I was supposed to be doing, I was crystal clear in denying it altogether. I said, "Give me a manual, and I'll learn it," but I had a feeling that it wouldn't be as easy as it used to be. After the interview, I waited for the answer, and when I knew that I got the position, the first reaction was of amazement. Once again, I felt that, behind that situation of trust, a new professional opportunity was hiding and I could not easily miss it.

I closed IT Consulting and a whole series of activities that I was carrying out and started working at Fastweb. So anyone who reads will surely have understood that, until 2008, I didn't know anything about automation. I didn't even know that there was anything with this strange name.

During my years in the company, I have never attended automation training courses. My knowledge and training on process automation have been all under the cap of "learning by doing", learning by trying and experiencing first-hand the great opportunities offered by automation. My first day in the new process automation office was unforgettable. I arrived at my desk very early, put my things on the table, and a few moments later I saw my boss coming. He took a flash drive out of his pocket, slipped it into my computer and pointed to the software inside. He explained to me that this was the software they used to make process automation and asked me to install it on my computer, try it out and let him know the next day how it went. Then, he

RPA for everyone – by Vincenzo Marchica

turned around and left, and that day I never saw him again. After the first moment of panic, I began to think. My heart was pumping with adrenaline because the man had just challenged me. And I love challenges. I installed the software, looked for a shred of manual online - which wasn't there - or something to explain how to make it work, and then I started to do some tests to build a little robot, a first self-taught automaton. I realized that already when I turned on the computer, there was the first possibility of automation, the first trigger: the automation could put for me, when I turned on the computer, username and password, and command to open Outlook autonomously. In a few minutes, I created the robot, wrote four lines of code, turned off the computer and tried to turn it on again to see if everything was going as I had described. Once I pressed on, I noticed that the laptop pressed by itself the Ctrl+Alt+Canc keys, entered the username and password, logged in, opened Outlook, opened the company system to pass the badge online, entered the start time and from there left me the PC ready to work. All of this without me moving a finger. For me, it was something revolutionary, the beginning of a new world, the discovery of the great potential of technology—all in a few minutes. The next day, my boss was happy to see my progress and showed me a robot that had already been made. Then he began to give me tasks, and I was fully immersed in the job.

The new office's main task was to automate the creation of company reports. The person responsible for that new creation, my boss, was the new head of reporting. His name is Roberto, and he was put in charge there with the clear target of automating everything possible. In the beginning, the new office was made up of Roberto and myself, so we did some tests to understand how

RPA for everyone – by Vincenzo Marchica

to handle the unique situation and the task we were given. It was an exciting start, as in just three months, we built the automation that was needed to produce all the reports that were being made at the time by the reporting team (4FTE).

We proceeded on our path so that all the processes related to any activation passed from human control to that of the automation we were creating. To do this, we needed several computers capable of continually monitoring the work the robot was doing according to the instructions we had given it.

The automation ran on our computers all night long. We managed to get the computers to stay on all the time, even when no one was going to the office. To prevent the cleaning ladies from touching them and eventually block the process, Roberto and I were careful not to leave keyboards and mice on the desks. When the "little automation" came up with some significant results, Roberto and I made them talk and tell us what they had achieved through the "text to speech", a short and straightforward text that showed us the level of work they had done - like, for example, "I'm starting the process...", or "I'm missing fifty". It happened, then, that some of our colleagues in the morning, passing by our office, heard someone inside talking and then asked us who we had segregated all night or all weekend working on our behalf. When, on the other hand, the automation reached significant flows or particularly long-awaited or complicated goals, the music of the "Ride of the Valkyries" from Stanley Kubrick's film "Apocalypse Now" started in the background. From this "alarm" we knew that the most awaited data had arrived. The more I worked alongside Roberto, the more I realized how strategically important the automation sector was, which at that time was still a "niche" sector, little known and little developed in the Italian corporate market. Working at Fastweb I understood that this type of work would be the future and that it was absurd to make so little use of it.

In almost five years at Fastweb we have automated more than 130 processes. Our area of intervention was "activation", the various techniques were intended for Customer Care to speed up and optimize activities for salespeople to analyze and manage agency and sales force sales. We also implemented processes for other groups and other functions. I certainly can't list them all, but I can assure you that they have brought enormous benefits to the company in both economic and quality terms and also in speed.

In early 2013 I was hired by a consulting firm called "Babel". This company used to manage various consultancies and projects with major clients of the Italian business reality. It happened that PosteCom asked them for an IT consultant, most known as a project manager, to work on some projects within the company. I saw this opportunity as the next step in my career. The economic proposal that Babel made me was too tempting to refuse. More benefits also meant more responsibility in project management, but I saw this as a small problem. The important thing was to be there to know that I had the confidence to do a good job there too.

This experience has given me a lot, I have learned how to manage more complex and more significant projects and above all how to manage many stakeholders simultaneously and on several fronts. During these years, I was constantly noticing projects that could be solved with RPA or where it could be introduced with great benefit both economically and in terms of time. But it was not yet the time, and my advice was not taken on board.

This continuous glimpse of automation everywhere convinced me after about three years to leave Babel and start my own business in the world of Business Process Automation. Which very soon I was going to call RPA!

Chapter 4 - The present: Vincix Group

My time at the Post Office had not extinguished my desire to resume working in the field of process automation, as I had done over the years at Fastweb. In the face of my great interest in automation, and in particular in Robotic Process Automation (RPA), although I was convinced of the practical usefulness of this model still unexplored in Italy, I realized that the people I was interfacing with did not have a clear vision of what automation was and, specifically, what RPA had to offer.

RPA was hardly mentioned at all and was often not appreciated... one day a vital manager of a big company said: what you tell me is only suitable for small companies... not in big companies like ours... I naively replied that it was used by major banks around the world and by giants 10/100 times bigger than his "big" company... but I understood that it was just a waste of breath...

When I resigned from the former Babel, I set myself the goal of fully working only on RPA projects. To do this, I needed some independence and a bit of madness and awareness of my means and abilities. A few months after leaving my previous job, I started working with the "Vincix Group" brand. My goal was to develop RPA projects, but with a company that did that only, with the great ideal of making RPA more known in the Italian market and being able to collaborate with big companies that really needed automation to survive the times of economic crisis and chronic lack of time to do everything.

The Vincix Group started out in a tiny location with 0 employees. Already at the end of 2016, I managed to move the office into a reasonably cheap room at Tecnopolo Tiburtino. My company was just born, and it was very small, but I knew that this would have been only temporary as accommodation before I settled somewhere else.

In the office at Tecnopolo I started to have a couple of employees who helped me set up the first projects and consultations. In a few months, the work was growing faster and faster, and we needed new staff and a bigger place to set up the developers. In mid-2017 I managed to find an office, the current one, in Viale Regina Margherita, right in front of Enel's headquarters. With the entry of new members on the Vincix Group's board of directors, the penultimate chapter of my professional experience was written. This took me around Italy, with different tasks, to my current identity, which identifies with the work I do every day for the Vincix Group, within that RPA system that is still so little known in Italy.

Since January 2018 my company has been working permanently in Italy and the UK. The first months were spent transferring all the contracts and projects from the old company to the new one, organizing the new office, enlarging the workforce and a whole series of bureaucratic procedures necessary to start a company in

RPA for everyone – by Vincenzo Marchica

Italy. The exponential growth of activities goes hand in hand with an increase in turnover. Despite the bureaucratic shifts and the "waste of time" in the various stages of the company, the Vincix Group closed 2017 with an active turnover as in 2018.

Chapter 5 - London, 2016

There is a date in my young life that I will not forget so easily after my marriage... it is the 14th of December 2016. It is an important date because starting from that moment, I have had the confirmation that the professional path I have undertaken in recent years was not a utopia, a personal fixation that has no positive results in the social environment I frequent, but a reality that was - and still is - slowly taking hold in Europe and the USA. I learned about an event organized by IRPA-AI, which at the time was only called IRPA, Institute of Robotic Process Automation, and I looked on the internet for more information on how RPA was seen abroad. I didn't think twice: I read the title and the program of the conference and decided to register for the event. On 14 December 2016, I showed up at the conference reception. Once inside, as I expected, I was attacked by a horde of salespeople trying to sell me their RPA solutions in order to do business more quickly and effectively. Every time I answered that, like them, I was one who was developing and implementing RPA solutions for clients, I was immediately snubbed, so I was left alone, and I was able to focus on how much that event could help me to improve my new profession.

I don't exaggerate in writing that, coming out of that event, I was excited. It was a typical English event, with just over two hundred and fifty people present. There was a talk about RPA, its future developments, success stories all over the world and, in the end, you could even think about having a chat with the speaker of those success stories. The talks started early in the morning and ended around five in the afternoon. From that time on, the open bar began, and people could exchange a few jokes and have a drink with those who had presented their reports in the morning, who were very willing to listen to the audience's questions and take a picture with all those who would have liked to. I had the opportunity to meet and exchange a few words with Frank Casale, the founder and president of IRPA-AI and a professional who has always worked to help society through technology. That event was too emotional and the certainty of having a beautiful profession.

Until that moment, I had never had the opportunity to explore the benefits of RPA in my country, because no one was aware of what was being done around the world on this topic. In a few hours there in London, I followed events where the founders and CEOs of many process automation companies, such as UiPath and Blue Prism, were exchanging ideas. I also had the opportunity to take a photo together with the great managers of these companies, a bit like going to a Fiat-Chrysler event in Italy and getting my picture taken with John Elkann. English and Indian people presence was the majority.

Figure 3 - With Frank Casale - IRPA AI event of 2016

This event triumphantly dedicated to what was called "the year of the robot", was something diametrically opposed to what was happening in Italy in terms of conferences: Italian conferences, including those that explore innovative technological aspects, continue to be boring, with people teaching from behind a table and explaining how they became so important. And when it is necessary to ask some in-depth questions to understand more, the Italian guru (usually a university professor) has already disappeared to go who knows where to hand down his verb. When the event came to an end, I was galvanized at the idea of being able to continue to develop that sector and attracted by the goal of making sure that even in Italy we began to talk about RPA in common and favourable terms. In my head, I felt that it was right to continue along the path I had undertaken because it was a valid, existing, full of possibilities and imaginative market.

RPA for everyone – by Vincenzo Marchica

It was only necessary to overcome the biggest obstacle, that is to make Italian customers better understand what this RPA was and how it worked. So, I worked hard to get to know those crazy people who, like me, had started working in the RPA world and then to set up an event similar to the one in London, to be replicated in Italy to make it an annual fixture, just like the one held by IRPA.

I got to know other people who were working in the sector, and I proposed to them to join us together to create an event to get to know and promote RPA in Italy. We were, after all, competitors who exceptionally joined together for a higher cause.

We created the RPA - Italy network, we associated and organized the first conference for 2017. As a venue we chose - look at that combination - the ELIS, which in that period followed with interest all the issues related to the "Industria 4.0" project. We added automation and innovation as a sector of knowledge and focus, and we were able to plan the day dedicated to the in-depth study of RPA for 9 May 2017. The event itself was half a fiasco: only about forty people attended, but they were really interested in the subject. Even though I was disappointed, I knew I had taken a small step: I organized the first conference on RPA in Italy. UiPath came to the conference and, given the low participation of the Italians, they decided to postpone their personal investment in the Italian market, leaving the start of the market to others.

The Italian conference in 2017 was followed by three other events, in May 2018 in Rome, September 2019, one in Milan and one in Rome. The London event of IRPA has had other editions both in the UK and the USA and is still a regular appointment for

RPA for everyone – by Vincenzo Marchica

those who want to learn more about Process Automation and Artificial Intelligence.

As far as I am concerned, the London experience also enabled me to have more significant relations with the most important RPA experts in the world and to promote interest in this growing sector in my own small way. This is how the RPA Hackathon organized by Vincix Group was born recently, in order to bring more knowledge of the phenomenon and to bring the youngest people closer to the world of RPA in order to start innovative start-up projects, able to make it easier and more common to use RPA projects not only for companies but also for interested individuals.

Chapter 6 - Exciting work

After having recounted the long journey that has brought me here, and before giving the reader an overview of the current potential of RPA, it seems fair to me to describe what my work consists of every day, a job that I carry out with increasing passion and with the knowledge that I will have it for a long time to come.

Now that companies in Italy, too, seem to have finally understood the role and importance of RPA projects in order to work more and better for the development of their business activities, we on the other side - and that we offer our professionalism in order to make them understand the great benefits of a well done RPA project - have the task of making ourselves available to encourage an increasing diffusion of automation.

25

My job is essentially to find, talk to and convince the potential client to rely on automation to leave part of their current work to a robot to do it in their name and on their own, without fear of losing out on total profits. It is a job that goes hand in hand with the more "routine" work of managing and developing existing projects, which have already started with various clients or are about to be launched shortly. The opening of a company and its consequent development has, of course, also imposed another line of work that I follow with growing enthusiasm and with no little effort: to grow a team of people who know how to work at my own pace and with increasing competence, training them as much as possible through the direct practice of the profession and in the concrete management of individual projects and specific clients. At Vincix we are working to have professionals who are not only technically good but also attentive to details and focused on problem-solving, and above all who never give up! I often tell my clients that we are like the Navy Seals, we don't leave any project behind, and we carry out every single mission.

Public relations have led me, over the years, to speak often to audiences to make them understand what RPA is and what it is not. I have spoken in front of more or less heterogeneous audiences, from established professionals to big business leaders, from university students to primary and secondary school children. In the last two years, I have seen and heard more or less absurd things about RPA. Many people pass themselves off as great RPA experts but, instead of conveying safe and truthful messages, they produce false myths that frighten clients and make an effort made by professionals to promote the use of RPA at all levels and under all conditions even for those who know nothing about it. When I talk to a client who is not aware of the

RPA for everyone – by Vincenzo Marchica

significant advantages that a good RPA project can produce in terms of costs and benefits, I realize that the problem is not so much in understanding what it is, but in the distorted perception of what can be done and what, instead, must be done. Not to mention a thousand doubts that arise when imagining how an RPA project can be done and what it means for the client in terms of modernizing the company's internal structures.

As far as the training of the team working in my office is concerned, I have no problem saying that - without mincing my words - this is something I absolutely cannot overlook. There are not many RPA developers in Italy, for the reasons I have already tried to describe above. The first problem, for me, is having to take young people with few skills to work here with me, having to train them and follow them carefully until they are entirely independent to follow a specific project. The second comes as a direct consequence of the first: when the young people who come here to work, they feel they are sufficiently trained and can move around even without being under the "Vincix Group" hat, they put their CVs in the right platforms, and within a few days they are already called by other companies. Just write on your LinkedIn profile that you are an "RPA developer" and the offers are constantly flooding in, so you are guaranteed a job. For me, however, it's the opposite. The moment a developer resigns, I have to run to get someone else to do the same tasks like the one who left, obviously without basic training.

I try not to miss moments when I try to show my team something important, and we try to organize brainstorming useful to grow in skills. One thing is sure: I am very demanding with new developers who come to Vincix to learn a job like this. In recent years I have

RPA for everyone – by Vincenzo Marchica

seen many young people crossing the threshold of my office. In teaching the work, there is a necessary first phase dedicated to learning what has to be done. You have to learn a new job and, for me, this means that it takes much more effort than average, it takes a lot of time and a lot of effort. You cannot behave like an established professional, but you have to be hungry to know the secrets of the job. Speaking of my work, I always expect a lot of commitment, dedication and the ability to sacrifice myself from a "young person". You can't feel arrived and ready the first day you start working in RPA. From a young person, I expect an attitude that shows humility, willingness to learn and goodwill.

I have always preferred people who, despite uncertainty and almost total ignorance, know-how to carry out a task to those who, despite knowing, have no desire to work hard to achieve a positive result.

Part Two

THE STRANGE JOB
Chapter 7 - RPA: What is it?

Technically, RPA, an acronym for Robotic Process Automation, goes beyond the simple idea of process automation as I had begun to do during my time at Fastweb. RPA means the use of different tools and platforms aiming at automating, through software robots, business processes characterized by well-defined and repeatable procedures on average structured data. These robots can automatically perform repetitive activities

RPA for everyone – by Vincenzo Marchica

"imitating" the behaviour of operators and interacting with computer application systems in the same way the human beings do their work. There is more: if automation was able to create robots that work essentially on well-structured data and mainly web applications, RPA has overcome this obstacle because the robot is also able to manage data from scanned documents, images or email texts and work on any graphic interface. I like to say that RPA robots are omnivorous.

When I give an explanation of what RPA is, I prefer to be essential and straightforward. In my opinion, the most convincing point from which to begin to understand what RPA is the one that, in some way, gives an initial indication of the role it can play for a single person: it is not a simple software that I install on a computer so that it does everything that is not humanly possible to do. On the contrary, I think of it as the "virtual colleague" who sits at the desk next to me and does the activities that a human being does not want to do or does not have enough time to do it.

Very often it happens that, in a company, some people are doing the same work over and over again for years or who, to hurry up and get it out of the way, does it with little skill and not in the best way. The worker may not realize this, but this way of working is damaging the company for three reasons: 1) a job that could have been completed earlier drags on for years and forces the company to slow down its business processes while waiting for that activity to be completed; 2) the company spends more money than expected, in terms of human resources and materials to carry it out, on a job that could have been completed much earlier and with minimal effort. 3) the quality and accuracy of the work are affected by a spot check rather than a sweep check.

RPA for everyone – by Vincenzo Marchica

By this, I don't mean that the robot is a perfect being and that it never makes mistakes. On the opposite, a robot behaves like a human being and can even make a few gross mistakes. I can, however, honestly say that a robot almost always manages to do a job in less time than a person would perhaps do more carefully, but by sacrificing days and days of work.

Another example I can give is indicative of the relationship between doing repetitive work and delegating it to a robot. I believe that the innovative scope of RPA in the world of professions and in the corporate market is equal to that which there has been in the past when we moved from manual bolting to the use of the electric screwdriver. Anyone who was in charge of bolting bolts in a company would not have been happy with the change that took place when the electric screwdriver was introduced. Many may have thought they would lose their jobs at the expense of a machine, but the smartest companies cannot just fire a person they put their trust in out of the blue. So, it usually happened that workers who were replaced by machines were given new tasks and new roles within the company. A promotion, not a dismissal then.

With a slight change of perspective, I believe that RPA presupposes a change of mentality on the side of those who run the company and on those who work there. I often hear it said that RPA only means "firing people", it is seen as the devil's tool to reduce human resources costs and to be able to overcome, in this way, the moments of crisis of the company, waiting for the calm after the storm. As I said before, a vision of this kind can also be legitimate by those who see it from the outside, but it does not correspond to the reality of the facts. RPA should be seen as the

RPA for everyone – by Vincenzo Marchica

act of putting a robotic entity (what I have already called "virtual worker") next to the employees already present to whom the most monotonous or repetitive jobs are assigned; those kinds of jobs which seem absurd a person could carry out for the rest of the life.

We are talking about enhancing the value of our employees by making them do what RPA robots are not able to do, such as negotiating with a customer or supplier, finding a creative solution to bureaucratic or technical problems, and, above all, capturing the emotional aspects that can lead to success in a deal or claim. There can be many examples, and I can't list them all but what I'm going to expose below can give you a concrete idea.

For instance, an employee of an insurance company who has to manage a claim, with the support of RPA and in this case also a pinch of AI, will find the file already "normalized"; the robot will have retrieved all the data necessary for analysis, will have made comparisons with similar files, will have searched for bureaucratic or legal problems and, eventually, it will give evidence of them, will have checked that all the documents are present and it will have automatically asked to be sent. All this will allow the human being to concentrate only on the resolution of the claim and will not have to waste time in what has already been done by the robot. In fact, the work will be more efficient, faster and above all, more satisfying for the person who will grasp its added value.

A robot does not complain if it is unsatisfied of his work, while for a human being this is often the first cause of depression or personal remission with respect to his own motivations or ideas of being able to do a job well done and with a minimum of pleasure. I have often heard complaints from companies about

RPA for everyone – by Vincenzo Marchica

relationships with suppliers. It is often the case that the purchasing department of a company comes into contact with suppliers very frequently and that so-called "document dances" can take place, whereby a supplier sends a specific document to the purchasing department, and the person working there realizes that the form is wrong. The person returns the form to the supplier. The supplier reads the message and sends back the document. The purchasing department notices that the document is right, but it has expired and must send it back to the supplier. The supplier receives the message, returns the document and this time the Chamber of Commerce view is missing. The purchasing office sends the document back with a hint of irritation...and the dance has made the person working in the purchasing office of that particular company lose at least a couple of days.

These are all activities that have added no value; they are just an endless nuisance. If there was a robot to supervise this type of activity, I think it would save us the hassle and annoying comments of those who have to follow these procedures to their perfect conclusion. The robot knows how to carry out these "boring" tasks in a proper way, and it never tires of doing them, if a document is incorrect it automatically sends it back two hundred times a day, if necessary. I can assure you that I have never seen or heard a robot puffing to do a job I had programmed it for. Even if a customer makes a mistake twenty times when sending a document, the robot will respond twenty times by pointing out the error. And I'm sure that, in the end, the robot will win, even if only because the distracted customer is exhausted. So, after having delegated all this endless ballet to the care of the

RPA for everyone – by Vincenzo Marchica

robot, the employee will have time to do other things to make the relationship more and more stable and definitive.

The robot that was built specifically for that task is schematic. Is it told to do one thing? He does it without complaining. The movie "Forrest Gump" comes to mind, when the character played by Tom Hanks remembers that he was a perfect soldier because when he was told to do something, he did it without wondering why, how and if it made sense. I think the robot at the heart of every RPA project for a company is like the perfect soldier described in the movie. On this point, when I talk to my clients and I'm at the point where I have to start the speech and present the activity we're about to design, I always say that I see the robot as a colleague to whom they want to put all the most obnoxious jobs, with the certainty that it will never send them to hell and it won't do any scratch to their car.

RPA, therefore, presupposes a change of mentality. This a change that touches deeply any entity, personal or corporate. As it can be seen from what has been said in these pages, RPA is useful both to the individual professional and to the entire company body. There is a need, however, for a predisposition to change.

Generally, when it comes to changing a process, a procedure or a way of working, you may have to deal with people who are trying to find various justifications to not go ahead with it or trying to hinder the change. The terrible sentence that freezes the blood in my veins when I hear it is: "this is how it has always been done! A sentence like this is a shield against any proposal for change. If a company goes into crisis because of "it' has always been like that", it means that that company has to ask itself a few more questions and understand that, in this way, it risks falling behind in time and

RPA for everyone – by Vincenzo Marchica

becoming less and less competitive compared to other companies in the same sector.

RPA is a sign of change. My main problem, in my daily work with clients, is to convince people to change and that the change, as I propose it to them, generates benefits. It is not just a matter of money or fear of the future: the biggest obstacle for RPA is precisely the lack of trust and courage of companies and individuals.

People who are not afraid of losing professional prestige, who are sure of their value, are the ones who have the most confidence in change. They know that they do a job that is easily reliable to a robot, but they are not afraid of it. On the contrary, they see the opportunity to give the job to a machine as the right opportunity to develop the second phase of their professional prestige, which they could not consider before due to lack of time. I know, from direct experience, that in Saudi Arabia RPA is strongly considered and developed not so much because in this way companies save on personnel, but because those who work want to leave the office earlier, work as little as possible to enjoy life, family, children, pastimes. This should be, also in Italy, the real prospect to invest in RPA projects and make it, in a short time, more common and easy to know, within everyone's reach.

RPA for everyone – by Vincenzo Marchica

Chapter 8 - RPA: why?

With all the premises developed in the previous chapter, it is clear what is the main reason for deciding to start with an RPA project. It promises significant savings in time and money. In the first aspect, "theoretically" RPA develops automatic software that can run continuously 24 hours a day, seven days a week, do not need any rest and do not lose concentration during prolonged work. As for the second aspect, looking specifically at the results of an RPA project, it is possible to achieve 100% reductions in labour costs in business processes, with negligible error rates in the performance of tasks and processes and therefore a significant increase in quality. All this, of course, if the designed automation is supported by a well-built, implemented and controlled RPA system.

In my experience as an RPA designer and developer, I have always noticed that the idea of automating a whole range of activities is a double-edged sword in the hands of a company: on the one hand, there is the need to take away so many tiring and boring tasks that can easily be delegated to a robot; on the other hand, however, there is the risk of realizing what the situation of a company really is, how many mistakes have been or are still being made in the management of specific processes, and how production could be increased and costs saved if only some ways of working could be changed.

I can say, without any doubt, that RPA helps companies to save even hundreds of thousands of euros a year and this depends essentially on two elements that are often overlooked: 1) the control over human activities;

RPA for everyone – by Vincenzo Marchica

2) the control of fraud and small errors that, added together, make companies lose a lot of money.

As far as the first point is concerned, the savings that come from relying on an RPA project all depend on the fact that a robot is entrusted with a job. The human operator, no matter how attentive and trained, gets to a certain point; our brain does not allow us to work continuously for many hours in a row, but we need a few breaks to recharge and resume work, a break to have a chat, the weekend to rest with the family, the Christmas and summer holidays, the simple night hours to recover from a hard and intense day...

The robot doesn't care about all this, because it tends to work no-stop until you say it. When a human being works in a repetitive way, it is expected that errors occur, even small and almost intangible ones. Regarding huge companies, it is clear that a mistake of a thousand euros is challenging to catch and even passes undisturbed; if however, that same company has a centralized and robotized system to control the activities carried out in a month, the errors will be easily highlighted. Twenty thousand euros errors that are avoided are a clear saving of a large amount of money. This is difficult for those who consider RPA a waste of time or a threat to their jobs to understand. It happened to me once, during a meeting where I was presenting a project, to show what I was going to implement in the company, I showed a robot in action. One person in the company, looking at the activity done automatically, came up and told me that she was much faster than the robot we had created. I said that wasn't the point... And I didn't want to argue against it. Usually, these

RPA for everyone – by Vincenzo Marchica

objections die out on their own in front of the statistics of a well-designed project.

On the second aspect, closely linked to the first, I can say that an RPA project done in the best way also helps to combat fraud against the company. An example of a few years ago is this: I was asked to create an automaton that would collect all the final figures of some suppliers and verify their correctness. The robot had to access various systems and carry out a series of checks in order to calculate its truthfulness. After a month of reviews, I had recorded something like twenty thousand euros of false results. We released the robot into production and extended the perimeter; that year, I saved the company just over three hundred thousand euros. This is a classic example to show that a well-done RPA project brings undeniable economic benefits.

Compared to automation projects carried out by IT offices, the advantage of an RPA project lies in its speed of execution and total duration (a project almost never exceeds three months), the simplicity of these processes and the low cost. All RPA projects can be started quickly, without lengthy previous analysis phases, do not require the involvement of IT professionals and experts, and no system integration activities are needed. These are elements that can easily convince the company of the need to automate processes through the use of a well-designed RPA.

Another benefit that RPA brings to companies is in terms of productivity. I have often started RPA projects in some companies despite the negative opinion of some managers and, once I came back to check how it was going, I noticed that the "opponents" were no longer working for that company. What had happened? Probably the increase in quality and quantity of work between

37

what was happening before RPA and after it (70-80%) was a sign that previously there was less work and low productivity. If a robot carries out one hundred practices per hour and the human being only ten, the disproportion is so high that one can wonder what that employee was doing in an hour. Of course, there can be a thousand reasons, but in that specific case, the RPA project revealed a great deal of disorganization.

Finally, as already written in the previous pages, RPA makes sense because it also allows improving the quality of life and work of people who are freed from the task of performing low-level and repetitive tasks over time. So, to sum up, the objectives and benefits of RPA are ethical, professional and economical in nature.

Chapter 9 - RPA: for everyone?

Readers might think: well, so RPA and its highly valuable services, in terms of economic savings and increased production, are essentially in favour of the most innovative companies and entrepreneurs to grasp the secrets to be able to excel in the national and international market... I would like, in these pages, to explain why I disagree with this thought. Or rather, I would like to expand it. I believe that understanding RPA as linked to corporate use is a "partial" vision of the phenomenon, a way of putting a label to easily wash your conscience and say that there is no margin of use for VAT professionals or private individuals. I agree that the first supporters of RPA come from within Business Process Outsourcing and financial services. However, the use of RPA can be favoured, for example, in some sectors, such as retail, energy, utilities, telecommunications and production systems. As mentioned above, RPA solutions are designed to allow a robot to perform the most common operations, those that a human being could perform with less and less attention because they are extremely repetitive over time. Some quick examples come to my mind: the approval of mortgages in the banking sector, order confirmations in the manufacturing industry or in the transport sector. The use of these solutions frees the time of human operators so that they are directed to different and more valuable activities, drastically reducing the time needed to complete the activities and the number of errors in the operations that are carried out.

My long and intense experience in the world of RPA leads me, however, to broaden this reflection and introduce a concept that

RPA for everyone – by Vincenzo Marchica

takes up an old quote from Bill Gates. The American tycoon, at the beginning of the massive development of computers, had a personal slogan in mind: "A computer for every desk". The meaning of this phrase was clear and meant the desire to control the whole world by having his own operating system installed on every computer. What was applicable for Windows and Bill Gates twenty years ago, could now be useful for RPA and its future. "One robot for every computer", this is the necessary step that RPA must take to be understood and appreciated. Even now, this phrase is no longer a distant fantasy, which is why I consider RPA to be a benefit for everyone and not just for the more enlightened and less afraid of change.

I'm talking about a type of automation that also concerns individual professions, the most well-known professional figures who can see, in RPA, an opportunity to speed up their work and be able to find time to follow an activity alongside the actual work, like for example studying something new.

I take the case of the profession of lawyer, an example that could be replicated for a thousand other jobs.

One of the activities of a lawyer, of course, is to inspect some documents produced by a court, as well as, sending documents to respect the deadlines of the trials he is following, both in civil and criminal matters. It is often the case that a lawyer has to do these tasks on his/her own, physically going to the court to read or deposit documents that are important for the resolution of the trial. The lucky ones, or at least those who can afford it, leave these tasks to a personal secretary, who takes up her time going and coming back from the law firm to the court and vice versa, and sometimes she also has to go to the post office to send the

RPA for everyone – by Vincenzo Marchica

documents. This is the reality of things. In my head, on the other hand, I see another possibility:

 that a robot can carry out these operations remotely, that it can take files from a folder and send them to the right e-mail address or that it can upload them to the court portal. If we think of the robot as a "virtual" helper working with you, this example of the lawyer's profession does not differ from what I have been saying for several pages now. The robot is a workmate who does the paperwork for you, who sends documents, who asks you whether or not to sign the documents, which opens the signature program, who prepares everything before sending it and asks you to confirm what he is sending. And while the robot prepares everything, the lawyer no longer has to think about that file and can devote himself to do something else, reading other documents, studying a case he has to face in court or simply resting with his family or friends.

I do not exclude, then, that it is the lawyer himself who created this little robot. A recent graduate who takes the qualification will definitely have this extra competence, because the more we go on over the years, the more computer skills will increase, even for those who have not graduated in Computer Science. I had to study and work long before I became an RPA expert, but the chromosomes were the same from childhood.

If I think about people who are absolutely incapable of doing technology, the picture is clear: previous generations do not have this ease of thinking in approaching such an innovative reality as RPA applied to services for the profession. I know many friends who work as teachers in the various grades of the Italian school. An elementary school teacher could use the RPA for himself, to

RPA for everyone – by Vincenzo Marchica

upload some specific files on the school portal, or to send a school assignment - a check - to his pupils, or to check if there have been changes in the school hours shift as indicated in the various official communications or not on the school website or on the company email. In this case, the robot does not have the function of remembering its appointments: the robot in the RPA is not like "Siri" or the "Google Ok" we use on our smartphones. In our devices, the voice assistant reads personal agenda and tells us what we have to do, while in the case of a robot in the RPA, the robot acts on an external computer and goes looking for information on an external site, which contains information about us and about what we want to know.

Of course, RPA is - at least on paper - within everyone's reach. I am, however, well aware that creating a robot cannot be the ultimate solution to a problem, especially if it concerns a profession such as that of a lawyer or teacher. It is not possible to automate the work, but you can automate all those jobs related to the profession, that series of "paperwork" that the professional cannot leave to his or her own fate, because they would prevent him or her from doing his or her job in the best possible way. For the lawyer, these "paperwork" is sending documents, signing, receiving e-mails, reading and scanning certain documents, analyzing databases, recovering important files in databases. Try asking a secretary if she is happy to do "only" those jobs...and then ask her employer if these side jobs - only apparently - are done at the right time. Even the best secretaries can take a day off, get sick and leave the office early, or take longer than expected. And if these activities are not carried out by the secretary for whatever reason, who will have to carry them out? The lawyer, of course... with the consequent loss of time and

RPA for everyone – by Vincenzo Marchica

slowdowns in the professional organization. The robot is not the solution; the human being could best do these jobs. But time stretches immeasurably, and you have no other daily objective, everything else takes second place.

You do not automate the profession, as much as the services to the profession, all that series of manual and practical activities that are far more boring which a person would do in a very long time and without particular enthusiasm.

A robot, as I said, is not the solution to all my problems. But what I am trying to instil in people is thinking about it, trying to see how to improve the way they work with this not inconsiderable help. It is an attitude, a choice that cannot go unnoticed, a sign of attention towards one's work and towards the future.

I recently took part in a conference where the links between RPA and artificial intelligence were discussed. We all agreed that the only work that a robot can never replace, or at least that will be very difficult to replace is the one that, within it, has a strong emotional charge, a very emotional human sphere. A robot can be programmed in the best possible way. It can be filled with functions and important tasks that it performs to perfection; it can really be the monstrous product of technology that can make even insiders' eyes peep out... but it can never have the relationship, the contact, the emotionality of a human being. The teaching profession can never be replaced by a robot. The emotional charge is too high. A teacher must be able to speak to his pupils not only with words but also with his eyes. Even if we replace the teachers with robots to explain the lessons, when a doubt arises in the student's mind, the robot will not stop to understand the doubt and will not explain to make itself better

RPA for everyone – by Vincenzo Marchica

understood. A robot can replace a teacher, for example, in the correction phase of a task, especially if the task is multiple-choice. Correcting a school theme is not a task that can be entrusted to a robot, because a is not only grammar but also a cultural expression of a child's emotions.

I have tried to explain, in a few words, why I fight every day to make RPA known to everyone. As a result, I would now like to point out what are the essential characteristics for which I feel I must promote the use of RPA in everyday life of both companies and individuals. When a client commissions me to develop a new software robot that responds to his desire to speed up a process and save a fair amount of money on the budget, the first thing I say to the guys in my team is always the same: we pretend that the robot we are going to create meets our personal needs. We have to make a robot for a customer thinking that, after all, we are making it for ourselves. Only with this in mind we can enter the customer's mind and solve the criticality he has indicated to us. That being said, I believe that there are at least five characteristics that RPA possesses that make it highly attractive to companies and individuals who need it.

The first feature is SPEED. I think it has already emerged how this characteristic is at the basis of every RPA project and responds to the wishes of all those who have turned to me in recent years to solve problems related to the length of some very costly business processes in terms of economic and human resources.

Speed, in this sense, wants to be the real incentive to choose a robot that "replaces" the human being in some functions. In its true meaning, however, speed lies in the fact that an RPA project does not last more than three months and that the central part of a project is the phase after the robot has been built, its implementation, the control of the work overtime.

There is a second feature linked to the speed, SIMPLICITY. Despite the misguided saying that developing an RPA project is complicated, the reality is that it takes very little to set up an RPA system capable of meeting one's needs. The RPA developer, in fact, programs very little. The real task of the RPA developer is to give a definite answer to his client on how to make it easier to carry out that task, whatever the workflow, the workflow behind that RPA system may be. Easy realization, then. The two features (speed and simplicity) are the real strength of RPA, especially in comparison with the first automation projects, those that were carried out at the end of the first decade of the 2000s. I a short time, RPA's systems will become so simple that it will be child's play to create a robot even for those who, at the moment, are not very familiar with the technology or use it only in a personal and ordinary way.

The third characteristic is NON-INVASIVITY. The only thing that changes when you use an RPA system is the fact that a robot does the work for you. There is no need to disrupt the systems in use in your company to adapt to RPA. You don't need to replace or modify the software, and you don't need to change your IT system, you don't need to expect the IT department to be aware of the changes that are taking place. What the company has today will also have tomorrow. But there will no longer be human beings

RPA for everyone – by Vincenzo Marchica

to carry out those activities. There will be a robot, and this robot will do what the entrepreneur asks of the RPA developer.

That's the point. The robot does not take any initiative of its own free will unless the implementation of the system deems it useful for the robot to be given more tasks than the initial level. And since all RPA projects are of short duration, the latter possibility is what becomes, in many cases, the ordinary reality.

The fourth feature is TRANSPARENCY. This word often lends itself to not being fully understood. When I speak of transparency, the concept has two possible unique meanings: on the one hand, there is the transparency of the activities carried out by the robot, so the customer always knows what is being done because, in addition to telling him or her about it and preparing the software that will then run on the virtual assistant's computer, he or she can see it directly, in the first person; on the other hand, transparency indicates that the work carried out by the robot has all the expected characteristics, so the customer does not care if the robot is working or not. The double meaning of transparency has a common element: RPA moves and always takes place in the sunlight, there are no secret details that only the developers know and there are no hidden frauds with the sole purpose of fooling the client on some particular aspect. I have already expressed in the first part - and I will most likely do so again in the next few pages - that RPA is designed and built to support the customer and not to deceive him. So, transparency is welcome if it succeeds in convincing the client of the goodness of RPA's projects and the need for its dissemination.

The last characteristic, which follows what has already been written for speed, is TEMPESTIVITY. A few years ago, digital

RPA for everyone – by Vincenzo Marchica

transformation projects were on everyone's lips because they were seen as an example of the future that was advancing. Today, thanks to RPA, that period is now an old memory, a mandatory step but which, thank God, is no longer current. Those projects were so complex and basic that the first results of the digital implementation could only be observed and captured after a minimum period of twelve months from the start of the project. It is unthinkable that a client could wait so long to see the results of his choice to innovate the way his company and some departments in particular work.

The results of an RPA project can already be seen after one month from the start, at the latest, after three. If I have to wait six months for a result means that the RPA project is not going well, that there are many bugs, that a good analysis phase has not been made before starting the project. Timeliness is the real obligation of an RPA project. It makes both software developers and entrepreneurs happy. In the age of "everything and now", RPA stands out because, if done well, it always delivers what it promises. If, in many cases, hurry is really a "bad advisor", for a company that wants to increase its productivity and not be overshadowed by its competitors in that particular market segment, then hurry is the daily bread to survive and show off before the public and its most loyal customers.

RPA for everyone – by Vincenzo Marchica

Chapter 10 - RPA: criticalities

Remember, all that glitters is not gold. This simple proverb, banal in its most essential meaning, also applies to RPA. Those who work on it every day know that there are many obstacles that must be overcome before an RPA project can be defined. Having to overcome those interferences creates a few small problems and lengthens the time it takes to implement projects. It is as if a mechanism suddenly jams without one being able to notice it in time.

What is blocking the development of RPA in Italy, for example, is a set of problems of various kinds: they are technical, economic, administrative and cultural problems. Starting from issues of a more technical nature, RPA cannot, in fact, assemble dozens of robots all together that are able to automate different and intersected processes. This is what is called a "scalability problem": it is easy to create a single robot that automates a process or a limited number of similar processes while it is more challenging to create an ecosystem of many robots put together. Statistics tell us that only a mere 10% of companies that have adopted RPA solutions have gone beyond the simultaneous creation of around fifty robots.

Another "technical" problem concerns the best tools and solutions to carry out an RPA project. Although automation is not an essentially new concept; RPA is only experiencing a phase of rapid evolution in the last three years. Like any ongoing evolution, the tools that can be chosen to do RPA are still in the renovation

RPA for everyone – by Vincenzo Marchica

phase and what may seem innovative, at the beginning of the project, maybe already old after three months. Personally, when I carry out RPA projects with some clients, often, the initial version of the robot I create must already be modified when entering the post-implementation control phase. So, six months later, I am already working on stage 2.0 or 3.0 of that software that I was asked for because I can see with my own eyes that it needs to be updated. When you update a tool, you have to be very careful about what you have already created because it is not absurd to think that an update (patch) of a platform can undermine all the RPA architecture that has been built laboriously and after a period of intense work and study. Jumping from technical to administrative problems, the nature of an RPA project needs every possible facility to install the virtual assistant on the computer that will work in place of the human being without any hiccups blocking its operation. If, as I have already written before, a robot must be able to work twenty-four hours a day, seven days a week, this means that I must be able to control that computer remotely and avoid unexpected blockages that frustrate all the work done so far.

Sometimes happens that, for example, while I am developing an RPA project, I have to install a virtual library or any program... to proceed with these installations I obviously need to have all the administrative rights to be able to act according to my work plan, without having to make requests to the employer continually. So, the case that I write has really happened, I often find myself in the situation of having to install Office on my computer, and I clash with company policies that prevent me from being able to install the writing program or Excel on the virtual machines. Although I do not understand the reason, I have to stop in front of this

RPA for everyone – by Vincenzo Marchica

temporarily insurmountable obstacle. The problems are many and concern every possible aspect of the robot's work. You cannot make the robot access to shared folders. You cannot create web pages, and you cannot freely consult certain types of databases, and so on and so forth. There is a long history of bureaucratic and administrative complications that are underestimated from the very beginning, so that even at the start of the projects unsuspected blockages arise, not even taken into account during the negotiations and exchanges of views in the first few days. I attended many meetings where the only topic was how to deal with and solve the thousands of bureaucratic problems that hindered the start of an RPA project.

 A good RPA project - and I believe that being able to define an RPA project as "good" is not such a trivial matter - has to face and solve, from the beginning, a series of exceptions, piece by piece, month by month. Bureaucratic problems slow down the implementation of the project. The risk is to go back to doing a project "the old-fashioned way", i.e. with endless months of analysis and a few weeks of development. An RPA project has to deal immediately with administrative problems and then technical issues with the medium. As I am now quite familiar with the direction an RPA project can take, this is the first topic I discuss with a client interested in using RPA in their company. I have concluded that the problems that arose during the project can be avoided at the root: it is not uncommon for my company to offer potential clients ready-to-use virtual machines, ready to use, which are arranged in the best possible way following all the typical indications of an RPA project. This possibility, in which we are the ones working on the machines and much more rarely the customer himself, allows us not to waste time when a thousand

RPA for everyone – by Vincenzo Marchica

problems come to light and will enable the customer not to lose competitiveness and market share.

The economic problems are those typical of a service that does not have many years of history and which, at present, is still unknown to many people—today, developing RPA software costs between fifteen and twenty thousand euros on average per year. At the moment, RPA service is fast, simple, timely, non-invasive, transparent and economical. Companies want to be on the safe side and save money where possible, so they need to be offered all the guarantees they need so as not to increase their budget further.

The Vincix Group has also tried to address this obstacle, trying to meet customers' needs. When we understand that the company, although willing, has no idea what the economic benefits of relying on an RPA project will be, it can rent a robot created by us. In this case, the robot is designed "as a service", and the Vincix remains the owner of the license, then renting the robot to the company willing to pay rent.

Obviously, we too must take advantage of the convenience of this agreement: a license of nine thousand euros can be repaid if we rent the robot to ten customers and at the price of one thousand euros each; if there are few tenants, we will lose out. By doing so, therefore, the customer no longer has to spend nine thousand euros of license per year, but only his thousand euros of rent. Everything I have written is suitable for the present situation. The RPA is not yet known, but as soon as it becomes familiar, agreements like the one described a few lines ago will no longer have any *raison d'être*. The lowering of the price will make the service more common. By the time that time comes, I will

RPA for everyone – by Vincenzo Marchica

probably already be doing something else in my life. Some people might think I am cheating, but all I want is for RPA to be spread as soon as possible and become a common ground for everyone, experts or not.

Finally, here are the cultural and organizational problems. The development of RPA in Italy raises complex administrative issues. Any automation impacts on the work of the people involved in automated processes, and this generates the resistance mentioned above to change. The cultural problem raised by some intellectuals about digital jobs and the digital workforce made up, among many others, of RPA projects, is the fear of losing their jobs and taking a fair share of "useless" workers out of the workplace.

RPA is seen as a trap that can reduce jobs by 50% and give companies breathing space. Many analyses indicate that RPA creates more jobs than it eliminates but this does not mean that all the rumours are unfounded. It is quick to say "let's put the worker back on tasks where he/she could make the most contribution". When the robot replaces the human being in a part of the tasks it previously had, the relocation of the worker to other tasks presupposes an organizational strategy on the part of the company such that the employee has a real possibility of being employed in another way.

Another organizational problem facing the company concerns quality control. To put a robot to perform a task, previously the responsibility of the human being does not mean leaving the robot to its fate and carving out, when possible, space for other tasks. Even in the most automated companies, the position of those who have to control the general work of an office or the people under their control remains stable.

RPA for everyone – by Vincenzo Marchica

If the robot is the virtual colleague who can also make mistakes means that the quality control of the work carried out cannot be abolished regardless. It is necessary to specialize and improve in the type of work carried out. The company plays a crucial role in this because it aims to make the most of its best employees who, due to the presence of the robot, no longer do their everyday work.

It is clear from what has been said in this chapter that RPA is still an evolution to be taken with the springs and how important it is to make everyone understand that the central focus of RPA is not so much on saving money as on the ethical aspect of helping people to carry out their work precisely and on time.

Chapter 11 - RPA: a daily commitment

After having explained many times what an RPA project is, what its characteristics are and the commitment hidden behind every aspect analyzed, I have to reserve a part of my writing for the description of the work that takes place in my office and how we follow the client step by step throughout the duration of an RPA project for the company concerned.

There are essentially ten phases to an excellent RPA project.

1.   Approach with the client.

This is the very first phase of the work. We make contact with a client who has shown willingness to take an interest in what RPA is and how he can use it in his daily work. We try to make them understand what RPA is and what role it can play in their work. The approach in question is midway between theory and practice. When we introduce ourselves to companies, I usually tell a few positive anecdotes - success stories - that serve to reassure the client, to make them understand that they can trust us.

2.   Customer's needs understanding.

In this phase, it is the client who opens up to us, who describes his real need, the one he wants to be able to give a solution to. A concrete example can be: the customer has to upload a certain number of DURC (tax compliance certificate) per month to his SAP (one of the management software most used by companies). This is a job that anyone could do. A job that a human being would perhaps do very carefully at first and then with less and less emotional participation. When we have a concrete need, which we think would be useful to analyze to see if it can be automated, we move on to the next phase.

3. Mapping of activities already completed.

First of all, we need to realize how the client is responding to the need he has indicated to us. We want to see what he does and how he does it. This is the analysis or assessment phase, which cannot go beyond the maximum of three weeks of work. In this phase, we go to draw what is already in place within the company, the AS-IS (as it is now). Understanding "as it is now" means, in concrete terms, working alongside the client, analyzing how much time he or she carries out the task he or she has asked to automate, various control and analysis activities that will then be useful in the next phase.

4. Analysis of what we can automate.

Once the previous phase has been completed, we map the process and try to figure out what to automate and where. So, if the process involves a dozen or so activities, we try to understand if they are all fully automated or if, within this long process, there are decisional steps that must be left to the human being. The effort of this phase is to think as if we were already in front of the robot, trying to understand what it could actually do. If the process involves a precise sequence of actions, we must try to think about how we can involve the robot within one of these sequences, giving it certain points and precise commands that respect the phases and sequences already standardized. This is the most delicate phase, at least at the beginning. It is the standardization and structuring of the process in a digital way, with the aim of making the human variables disappear or

RPA for everyone – by Vincenzo Marchica

decrease. With this last result, we can advance one step in the realization of our work in favour of the client.

5. The first proposal for automated activities.

If before there was a necessary phase in which we have analyzed the current activities carried out by the client when the robot is conceived in its basic functions, we propose it to the client, showing the "TO-BE" (what it will be). This is a first approach to the functions that the robot will perform, so it is necessary for the client to begin to get a good understanding of how his activity will benefit him by analyzing how this robot will perform its tasks.

6. The client compares the two activities (AS-IS/ TO-BE).

Once the proposal has been made, the customer begins to evaluate the robot's work in order to understand where the advantage lies. It is important, in this phase and in the previous one, to let the customer experience the speed with which the process runs through RPA's tools. Obviously, the two activities (the one carried out previously and the one the robot will do) will have to have points in common, moments in which the two actions carried out by the human being and the robot will match. Beginning, critical points of the application and end of the process must necessarily match: to give an example, if the process carried out by the human being provides for a list of data to be taken from SAP, the robot will also take these same data from SAP. It may happen, at most, that if the robot realizes that those same data are present in a shared folder already downloaded, it will no longer take the data in SAP but will extract them from that folder.

RPA for everyone – by Vincenzo Marchica

The technical tool is different, but the start of the process has been respected.

7.   List of benefits of RPA activity for the company.

The proposal has been made. The customer has seen how the robot will perform that function and has been able to see the automation in operation according to the criteria agreed with the developer. Now is the time to push the accelerator and try to bring the customer on our side, energetically, and this can only be done by listing the benefits of this activity under the RPA cap. The benefits, I have already written in the first part, but it is good to remember them here, are essentially about time, precision, correctness, money-saving. The most tangible benefits are those concerning time and economic savings; it is less easy to understand what kind of benefits you will have in terms of precision. Before starting with the full development of the robot, in fact, the customer can only make an assessment of the time saved in doing that job and the economic benefit for his pockets. It is clear that, at least at the beginning, the customer essentially looks at the economic side. It is right that it should be so because developing an RPA project - at least for now - is an investment (not too costly) that requires foresight and confidence in the medium that goes beyond any possible reasoning. I believe, however, that the most important benefit, the one that I believe should be given more weight, is that - often not considered or simply not of immediate value - of the correctness of the work done, that is the quality of the task performed. Usually, an RPA project reduces the amount of error made by human beings by 70%. A substantial percentage, not to be hidden and not to be taken for granted. The only way the client can quantify the benefit

RPA for everyone – by Vincenzo Marchica

of the correctness of the work done is to relate the quality of the work to possible penalties in case of loss of time: if a job is done in a longer time than expected, and the fine for the delay is fixed, if I have a benefit of time thanks to the RPA activity, I know that I will not face penalties and I will save a fixed fee. In the same way, in addition to time, the benefit of having done an excellent job, without errors, is also quantifiable with the amount of money I save in case of failure to make an error. If a mistake costs me one hundred euros, having avoided even ten errors means a total benefit of one thousand euros. This is the reasoning that drives the client to start with RPA, except in cases where other factors slow down the start of work (as already written in the chapter in this part on RPA's "criticalities").

8.   Acceptance of the proposal.

At this point, the client has all the cards in his hand to be able to assess what he has to do and what he has to decide. The approval obviously concerns what has been planned in the "to be" phase. Once the client's consent has been obtained, our real work begins.

9.   Development of the software for the process to be automated.

The people who work in my office, the younger ones but also me and my "senior" colleagues, we are all developers, and we work mainly on automation projects. What does "software development" mean? It means that you always have to start from the customer's needs in order to create a specific software capable of carrying out the tasks to be automated. Large companies still act the old-fashioned way - and therefore fail to fully understand today's RPA phenomenon - when they first decide on the software regardless of the process to be automated. This is a big mistake: first, they have to understand how the process to be automated runs and then choose the software that best suits those needs. You open the RPA software and start programming. I borrow the term "programming", because it is a term that unites all types of software development, even if the development of RPA software is more visual than written. My developers don't spend days and days writing code, but they rely on the workflows (workflows) that that robot will have to carry out in order to carry out that particular process and make it intuitive. It is important, when programming in RPA, not

RPA for everyone – by Vincenzo Marchica

to focus only on the function of the process, but to be aware of the whole activity as a whole. Is the function to take a file from a portal and move it to another point? Well, it is a starting point, but it cannot be the only goal of RPA programming. You need to have in mind the idea of how the whole process should run. Otherwise, you risk not giving sure answers and only completing half the work. The idea of RPA is linked to the concept of finding the solution rather than studying the technicalities to achieve it. The old programming started from a datum, analyzed the function to be carried out and brought it to completion, often striving to write complicated and inconceivable codes and codices. RPA is much more creative. I have a function, inserted in a certain process. I have to look for the best solution, not the fastest one. The fastest solution is not the answer RPA is aiming for. An RPA project tends to give a better solution in terms of stability and not just speed. It has often happened to me to make RPA software with crazy rpm before arriving at the final solution. If to go from A to B I don't need to go through C, in RPA sometimes I need to go from A to C, then maybe even D and then I get to B, a different, more stable and not necessarily a lot of extra time wasted. In the RPA, you have to go beyond the only viable route, have a lot of patience and know-how to add laps without weighing down the robot created. This is the aspect I like most about the work I do now. I never get bored.

RPA for everyone – by Vincenzo Marchica

10.   Robot delivery and activity monitoring.

The Robot is ready. The customer is happy. He is given the work of weeks and can finally start with the automation. Have we finished our work? Not by a long shot. It is now that the most delicate phase begins. Just as for a writer, the most delicate phase is the revision of the first draft of his novel, so for an RPA developer, problems arise when his "creature" comes into action. The problems will be minor in the monitoring phase, and the more careful one is in the analysis phase to understand what the changes in the way of working or in the client's needs might be. It is only in the "post", in fact, that we can intervene to improve some essential aspects of automation. Activity monitoring is the longest part of the entire RPA software development process. I always tell my clients that if you start in a given month of the year, after three months, the initial version will have to be updated and will be different from the one in production, and after a year it will have already changed a third time. Clients initially don't believe it, but then they have to resign themselves to the fact that it goes exactly the way I described at the beginning.

An example of a change in progress, in the monitoring phase, is what I describe. Let's pretend that the process to be automated is to download some data from SAP. The data extraction works well for six months, and then it starts to fail by "time-out". What happened? The data to download has probably become a lot, too much for one extraction. If it used to be a hundred records, now there are two thousand. What to do? One possible solution is to take the extraction and "split" it into several parts, i.e. instead of just one "heavy" extraction, have the robot make small extractions with a few records at a time. Here, this is an example of a workaround, necessary in the automation phase of that particular process. It all takes place in the monitoring phase because we had not seen this problem before.

I always tell my guys that the first talent of an RPA developer has to be problem-solving: they have to be creative. Creative is not just a graphic designer. To solve problems, you need a lot of creativity, positive nature and highly developed practical intelligence. In RPA, it is essential always to find new solutions, so as not to get stuck on replicating what has already worked for a client. The problems are of various kinds, and each project has a problem rate of up to almost fifty per cent. I would only be selling RPA without it, losing sight of the concreteness of this endless and beautiful work.

Chapter 12 - RPA: the next developments

I like to make perspectives on the future. Certainly, the RPA phenomenon is at the height of its development, and I am sorry that in Italy, it has only been starting to be talked about for a couple of years. It is undeniable that, over the last few years, RPA has become increasingly popular in the market and will continue to do so in the future.

Some estimate that demand for robotic automation by 2024 will grow exponentially compared to today and that forty per cent of large companies will have real automation centres. McKinsey Global Institute says it will be possible to automate up to thirty per cent of the tasks that affect sixty per cent of a worker's time today.

And yet, despite all these rosy predictions, I am convinced that in five years' time, even today's RPA instruments will change. Perhaps there will not even be any more talk of RPA, so much so that some people now associate it essentially with artificial intelligence. In five years', I probably won't even be doing this work anymore: we will see how the future will change, and we will invent something new. The fact is that, like all good things, RPA will become commonplace. It will be so much used that we will have to invent something more to make it more attractive. It will become increasingly widespread and, sooner or later, most of the activities that are easy to automate or easy to think about will become so. It is always a question of relating costs to opportunities or the desire to automate.

If I had to imagine myself and my company five years from now, I would see it more different in nature than it is today. We will

RPA for everyone – by Vincenzo Marchica

probably become more and more manufacturers of artificial intelligence solutions; we will produce robots in series that will be sold "on the shelf" and companies will use ready-made robots in their processes. What's more, I'm convinced that the spread of RPA will be so vast and of great proportions that every person will be able to set up a robot for their computer. In companies, it will be possible for every employee to have a robot installed on his or her computer and the central offices will only be responsible for checking and controlling the robots' operation.

I know, it sounds like an Asimov vision, but behind these convictions of mine, there is the certainty that development is well underway and the promises to build the future are within our reach. And I can say this with certainty by looking back at how the tools that were once the domain of the few and are now within everyone's reach have spread. Nobody thought that apps for our smartphones would be so easy to create and implement: at the beginning, people who made mobile apps were considered one of the most inveterate scientists in the world, whereas today anyone could create one. No one thought that a program like Office would become so fundamental for everyone, and at the beginning, it was the domain of a few: then, however, the software spread, everyone became aware of it and started using it, and now it seems an irreplaceable tool. The same thing is being done with RPA software: to spread it as much as possible so that it will soon become commonly used, able to gain more and more market share. RPA developers are increasingly present on the market, whereas before they were a rare commodity. To understand how common RPA has already become, just go to the sites of the leading developers: UiPath, Automation Anywhere and HelpSystem give all users the possibility to download a free

RPA for everyone – by Vincenzo Marchica

or temporary version of their software that everyone can use on their computer. Then, however, in order to advance to the next level, you need to buy a specific license. So, from Bill Gates' phrase "one computer for every desk", we are moving on to its evolution, "one robot for every computer", faster and faster.

The only obstacle today is high costs. As long as RPA instruments remain high in price, its diffusion will be minimal. As soon as the diffusion is higher, and the novelty element will no longer be such, the cost will fall, and it will be easier for everyone to use it. In part, this lowering of prices is already a reality, if you consider the fact that the Vincix Group makes some Robots available for "rent" to customers. It is only a matter of a few years.

The real challenge for the future is to ensure that companies talk openly about how they use RPA in their processes and that all employees in a company are trained to create their own personal robot and use it in the tasks entrusted to them. The massive use of RPA will be the result of basic training, so companies will rely on every employee being prepared to do his or her job with the help of a robot created and developed by him or her. I imagine, for example, that the person in charge of mail dispatching can do this by installing a robot instead of calling the IT office for help. It's an important change of mentality, and I'm sure the time will come when we'll be working in a different way to what we're already doing today. Also, I think the real goal for the next few years is to automate companies' core business processes, not just their side activities. To explain it better, I would like a company or a company that is in charge of taking care of the payrolls of employees of a particular company to be able to use RPA automation to carry out its mission. Automating the whole

RPA for everyone – by Vincenzo Marchica

process, from start to finish, is what some telephone or banking companies are starting to do in order to attract new customers. It is the very concept of automation that takes on a new meaning.

In regards to this, the other challenge concerns the younger generations. I am very pleased to know that in some schools, STEM subjects are starting to be taught, even though STEM programming is more oriented towards procedural robotics, applied computer science. But surely there is the fact that, even if they are not the same thing, these teachings prepare the student to have an open mind to change, to discover new ways of proceeding and living. There are also RPA courses in schools around the world. These courses aim to teach our own work to the younger generation so that RPA becomes increasingly common over time.

Finally, I would like to say a few words to explain what the legal implications might be for a client's "wrong" use of a robot. Like everything that becomes everyday use, normality requires that there is a respectful use of the automated tool so as not to fall into legal aspects of a more penal-administrative than civil nature. Until now, there have been no legislative interventions regarding process automation. I am convinced that, given the common scope of the phenomenon and the many "claims" aspects of RPA, trade union rather than legal issues will soon arise. Those who are afraid of losing their jobs at the expense of a computer will try to protect themselves by going to the appropriate offices. Many people think RPA seems to be just a way of firing employees, I believe there will soon be legal rather than legislative action on the issue, and it is right that some pronouncements should also

RPA for everyone – by Vincenzo Marchica

help those working in the industry to understand that you can only move within certain limits.

The problems, in my opinion, will be more about the control of robots and the responsibility of those who programmed them when they go to perform "delicate" tasks where no margin of error can be present. I, therefore, believe that two aspects should be given importance: the control of the robot and the verification of what is developed, a sort of certification of the activities carried out by the robot in automation. It is clear that, when we go to build a robot for a customer when we think about the workaround, we must bear in mind that the operations carried out by the robot cannot be free and irresponsible, but must be aimed at carrying out the process and achieving the set objective. It has happened in the past that some agreements with particular clients have provided for financial or administrative damages, whereas it has never happened that the possibility of committing criminal offences has been contemplated. How to behave in this way? My answer is simple: if the robot is asked to perform a task with high criminal responsibility, I must either prevent the robot from doing that task or I must carry it out with a whole series of additional controls that will allow it to face a certain responsibility knowing full well the risks involved.

The massive use of RPA will undoubtedly increase the risk of these issues, often related to privacy rights. The time will come, therefore, when RPA will have to submit itself to the control of the law; for now, everything still flows in full freedom and "ethical" responsibility on the part of those who, like me, are committed to making life easier for others. Everything that will

RPA for everyone – by Vincenzo Marchica

come, as Lucio Battisti used to sing, "We will discover only by living".

Conclusions

Here we are, then, at the end of the route. In these pages, I have tried to summarise my professional experience and the characteristics of the work I do every day with increasing attention, trying to iron out criticisms or misunderstandings about the RPA phenomenon. I don't know if I succeeded, but I think the best pages are the ones I haven't written yet, the ones I will live in the next few years once I have passed the "forty" mark.

I want, however, to leave the reader one last pill about what I do and how I do it, leaving the floor to the children and young people for a moment. In fact, it often happens that I go around talking to young people about the work I do, and the question is always: what do you do for a living? This is the same question that my children ask me when they are at home. I have to give an answer, and I have to make them understand in a few words and using simple concepts what I have tried to write in these few hundred pages. How do you do it?

I have told my children that I make little robots that perform activities that human beings do not want to do or do not like to do because they are repetitive and boring. And I make these little robots that behave in the same way as people, replicating on the computer what they should do manually, thus doing the same things: a simple definition, perhaps the best synthesis of all this book. After I finished talking, I was silent, waiting for some reaction to what I said. The reactions came and, as always, amazed me.

One of my children has highlighted the social aspect of my work, the negative aspect that too many people in Italy still point out with a hint of annoyance: by doing these robots I would practically be taking many people out of work. The other, on the other hand, highlighted the practical, and therefore optimistic, aspect: with my robots, people would not have to do tedious work. So that's what my synthesis of their innocence has achieved. Now, I don't remember whether the practical aspect was highlighted by my daughter or my son, but I wouldn't be surprised if this vision is the result of the female brain, much more pragmatic than the male one.

The sunny aspect is the starting point I put before my eyes when I talk to a client: if I can make my interlocutor understand that the purpose of my work and his choice has this aura imbued with optimism, I have already won the game, and I can build on a solid foundation without the fear of having to jump a thousand obstacles. This is what I wish to all the people who do a job as beautiful, intense and profitable as mine: always be optimistic, always be positive!

RPA for everyone – by Vincenzo Marchica

Picture 4 With Frank Casale e Giovanni Sestili - Londra 2018

RPA for everyone – by Vincenzo Marchica

Picture 5 With Giovanni Sestili - BP World London 2018

Picture 6 Flying to London - 2018

RPA for everyone – by Vincenzo Marchica

Picture 7 RPA Congress in Berlin - Nov 2019

Picture 8 Convention in China - August 2019

RPA for everyone – by Vincenzo Marchica

Picture 9 with Frank Casale in Stockholm 2020

RPA for everyone – by Vincenzo Marchica

Appendix

RPA son Wikipedia

(text exported from Wikipedia, the free encyclopedia, https://en.wikipedia.org/wiki/Robotic_Process_Automation,url consulted on 11 December 2019)

Robotic process automation (or RPA) is a form of business process automation technology based on metaphorical software robots (bots) or on artificial intelligence (AI)/digital workers.[1] It is sometimes referred to as software robotics (not to be confused with robot software).

In traditional workflow automation tools, a software developer produces a list of actions to automate a task and interface to the back-end system using internal application programming interfaces (APIs) or dedicated scripting language. In contrast, RPA systems develop the action list by watching the user perform that task in the application's graphical user interface (GUI) and then perform the automation by repeating those tasks directly in the GUI. This can lower the barrier to the use of automation in products that might not otherwise feature APIs for this purpose.

RPA tools have strong technical similarities to graphical user interface testing tools. These tools also automate interactions with the GUI and often do so by repeating a set of demonstration actions performed by a user. RPA tools differ from such systems in that they allow data to be handled in and between multiple applications, for instance, receiving an email containing an invoice, extracting the data, and then typing that into a bookkeeping system.

RPA for everyone – by Vincenzo Marchica

Historic Evolution

The typical benefits of robotic automation include reduced cost; increased speed, accuracy, and consistency; improved quality and scalability of production. Automation can also provide extra security, especially for sensitive data and financial services.

As a form of automation, the concept has been around for a long time in the form of screen scraping, which can be traced back to early forms of malware. However, RPA is much more extensible, consisting of API integration into other enterprise applications, connectors into ITSM systems, terminal services and even some types of AI (e.g. Machine Learning) services such as image recognition. It is considered to be a significant technological evolution in the sense that new software platforms are emerging which are sufficiently mature, resilient, scalable and reliable to make this approach viable for use in large enterprises[2] (who would otherwise be reluctant due to perceived risks to quality and reputation). A principal barrier to the adoption of self-service is often technological: it may not always be feasible or economically viable to retro-fit new interfaces onto existing systems. Moreover, organisations may wish to layer a variable and configurable set of process rules on top of the system interfaces, which may vary according to market offerings and the type of customer. This only adds to the cost and complexity of technological implementation. Robotic automation software provides a pragmatic means of deploying new services in this situation, where the robots simply mimick the behaviour of humans to perform the back end transcription or processing. The relative affordability of this approach arises from the fact that no IT new transformation or investment is required; instead, the software robots simply leverage greater use out of existing IT assets.

Deployment

The hosting of RPA services also aligns with the metaphor of a software robot, with each robotic instance having its own virtual workstation, much like a human worker. The robot uses keyboard and mouse controls to take actions and execute automation. Normally all of these actions take place in a virtual environment and not on screen; the robot does not need a physical screen to operate, rather it interprets the screen display electronically. The scalability of modern solutions based on architectures such as these owes much to the advent of virtualization technology, without which the scalability of large deployments would be limited by the available capacity to manage physical hardware and by the associated costs. The implementation of RPA in business enterprises has shown dramatic cost savings when compared to traditional non-RPA solutions.[3]

There are, however, several risks with RPA. Criticism include risks of stifling innovation and creating a more complex maintenance environment of existing software that now needs to consider the use of graphical user interfaces in a way they weren't intended to be used.[4]

RPA for everyone – by Vincenzo Marchica

Impact on employment

According to Harvard Business Review, most operations groups adopting RPA have promised their employees that automation would not result in layoffs.[5] Instead, workers have been redeployed to do more interesting work. One academic study highlighted that knowledge workers did not feel threatened by automation: they embraced it and viewed the robots as team-mates.[6] The same study highlighted that, rather than resulting in a lower "headcount", the technology was deployed in such a way as to achieve more work and greater productivity with the same number of people.

Conversely, however, some analysts proffer that RPA represents a threat to the business process outsourcing (BPO) industry.[7] The thesis behind this notion is that RPA will enable enterprises to "repatriate" processes from offshore locations into local data centers, with the benefit of this new technology. The effect, if true, will be to create high-value jobs for skilled process designers in onshore locations (and within the associated supply chain of IT hardware, data center management, etc.) but to decrease the available opportunity to low skilled workers offshore. On the other hand, this discussion appears to be healthy ground for debate as another academic study was at pains to counter the so-called "myth" that RPA will bring back many jobs from offshore.[6]

RPA actual deployment

- Banking and Finance Process Automation
- Mortgage and Lending Process
- Customer Care Automation
- eCommerce Merchandising Operation

RPA for everyone – by Vincenzo Marchica

- OCR Application
- Data Extraction Process

Impact on society

Academic studies[8][9] project that RPA, among other technological trends, is expected to drive a new wave of productivity and efficiency gains in the global labour market. Although not directly attributable to RPA alone, Oxford University conjectures that up to 35% of all jobs may have been automated by 2035.[8]

There are geographic implications to the trend in robotic automation. In the example above where an offshored process is "repatriated" under the control of the client organization (or even displaced by a Business Process Outsourcer from an offshore location to a data centre, the impact will be a deficit in economic activity to the offshore location and an economic benefit to the originating economy. On this basis, developed economies – with skills and technological infrastructure to develop and support a robotic automation capability – can be expected to achieve a net benefit from the trend.

In a TEDx talk[10] hosted by University College London (UCL), entrepreneur David Moss explains that digital labour in the form of RPA is not only likely to revolutionize the cost model of the services industry by driving the price of products and services down, but that it is likely to drive up service levels, quality of outcomes and create increased opportunity for the personalization of services.

In a separate TEDx in 2019 talk,[11] Japanese business executive, and former CIO of Barclays bank, Koichi Hasegawa noted that digital robots can be a positive effect on society if we start using a robot with empathy to help every person. He provides a case study of the Japanese insurance companies – Sompo Japan and Aioi – both of whom deployed bots to speed up the process of insurance pay-outs in past massive disaster incidents.

Meanwhile, Professor Willcocks, author of the LSE paper[9] cited above, speaks of increased job satisfaction and intellectual stimulation, characterising the technology as having the ability to "take the robot out of the human",[12] a reference to the notion that robots will take over the mundane and repetitive portions of people's daily workload, leaving them to be redeployed into more interpersonal roles or to concentrate on the remaining, more meaningful, portions of their day.

Robotic process automation

Robotic process automation 2.0, often referred to as "unassisted RPA" or RPAAI,[13][14] is the next generation of RPA related technologies. Technological advancements and improvements around artificial intelligence technologies are making it easier for businesses to take advantage of the benefits of RPA without dedicating a large budget for development work.

While unassisted RPA has a number of benefits, it is not without drawbacks. Utilizing unassisted RPA, a process can be run on a computer without needing input from a user, freeing up that user to do other work. However, in order to be effective, very clear rules need to be established in order for the processes to run smoothly

RPA for everyone – by Vincenzo Marchica

Hyperautomation

Hyperautomation is the application of advanced technologies like RPA, Artificial Intelligence, machine learning (ML) and Process Mining to augment workers and automate processes in ways that are significantly more impactful than traditional automation capabilities.[16][17][18] Hyperautomation is the combination of automation tools to deliver work.[19]

Gartner's report notes that this trend was kicked off with robotic process automation (RPA). The report notes that, "RPA alone is not hyperautomation. Hyperautomation requires a combination of tools to help support replicating pieces of where the human is involved in a task.

Outsourcing

Back office clerical processes outsourced by large organisations - particularly those sent offshore - tend to be simple and transactional in nature, requiring little (if any) analysis or subjective judgement. This would seem to make an ideal starting point for organizations beginning to adopt robotic automation for the back office. Client organisations may choose to take outsourced processes back "in house" from their Business Process Outsourcing (BPO) providers, thus representing a threat to the future of the BPO business,[21] or whether the BPOs implement such automations on their clients' behalf may well depend on a number of factors.

Conversely however, a BPO provider may seek to effect some form of client lock-in by means of automation. By removing cost from a business operation, where the BPO provider is considered to be the owner of the intellectual property and physical implementation of a robotic automation solution

RPA for everyone – by Vincenzo Marchica

(perhaps in terms of hardware, ownership of software licences, etc.), the provider can make it very difficult for the client to take a process back "in house" or elect a new BPO provider. This effect occurs as the associated cost savings made through automation would - temporarily at least - have to be reintroduced to the business in order to whilst the technical solution is reimplemented in the new operational context.

The geographically agnostic nature of software means that new business opportunities may arise for those organisations who have a political or regulatory impediment to offshoring or outsourcing. A robotised automation can be hosted in a data centre in any jurisdiction, and this has two major consequences for BPO providers. Firstly, for example, a sovereign government may not be willing or legally able to outsource the processing of tax affairs and security administration. On this basis, if robots are compared to a human workforce, this creates a genuinely new opportunity for a "third sourcing" option, after the choices of onshore vs offshore. Secondly, and conversely, BPO providers have previously relocated outsourced operations to different political and geographic territories in response to changing wage inflation and new labor arbitrage opportunities elsewhere. By contrast, a data centre solution would seem to offer a fixed and predictable cost base that, if sufficiently low in cost on a robot vs human basis, would seem to eliminate any potential need or desire to relocate operational bases continually.

RPA for everyone – by Vincenzo Marchica